Growing Up

Seed to Apple

by Jodie Shepherd

EXPLORE the LIFE CYCLE!

Content Consultant

Diane Turner, Program Assistant
Purdue Horticulture Department
Purdue University

SCHOLASTIC

Library of Congress Cataloging-in-Publication Data
Names: Kimmelman, Leslie, author.
Title: Seed to apple / Leslie Kimmelman.
Description: New York: Children's Press, an imprint of Scholastic Inc,
    2021. | Series: Growing up | Audience: Ages 6-7. | Audience: Grades K-1.
    | Summary: "This book introduces readers to the life cycle of an
    apple"— Provided by publisher.
Identifiers: LCCN 2020031767 | ISBN 9780531136942 (library binding) | ISBN 9780531137055 (paperback)
Subjects: LCSH: Apples—Life cycles—Juvenile literature.
Classification: LCC SB363 .K555 2021 | DDC 634/.11—dc23
LC record available at https://lccn.loc.gov/2020031767

Produced by Spooky Cheetah Press. Book Design by Kimberly Shake.
Original series design by Maria Bergós, Book&Look.

Printed in Heshan, China 62

SCHOLASTIC, CHILDREN'S PRESS, GROWING UP™, and associated logos are trademarks and/or registered trademarks of Scholastic Inc.

1 2 3 4 5 6 7 8 9 10 R 30 29 28 27 26 25 24 23 22 21

Scholastic Inc., 557 Broadway, New York, NY 10012.

Photos ©: 1 grass and throughout: Freepik; 17: Phil Savoie/Minden Pictures; 18-19 branch: Freepik; 20 top: Peterfactors/Getty Images; 21: Paul Sawer/Minden Pictures; 24: Mahroch/Dreamstime; 26 center right: Thodonal/Dreamstime; 26 bottom left: BehindTheLens/Getty Images; 27 top: Island Images/Alamy Images.

All other photos © Shutterstock.

Table of Contents

Apple

This is the fruit of an apple tree.

Leaves

Leaves make food for the tree.

Trunk

The hard stem of the plant is called the trunk.

Bark

Bark helps protect the tree.

A Special Tree

This beautiful tree is filled with apples! It is an apple tree.
Like all trees, an apple tree is a woody plant. It has a stem and leaves. An apple tree is **deciduous**. Its leaves fall off in autumn and grow back in spring. The apple tree also has **blossoms**. Each blossom can grow an apple.

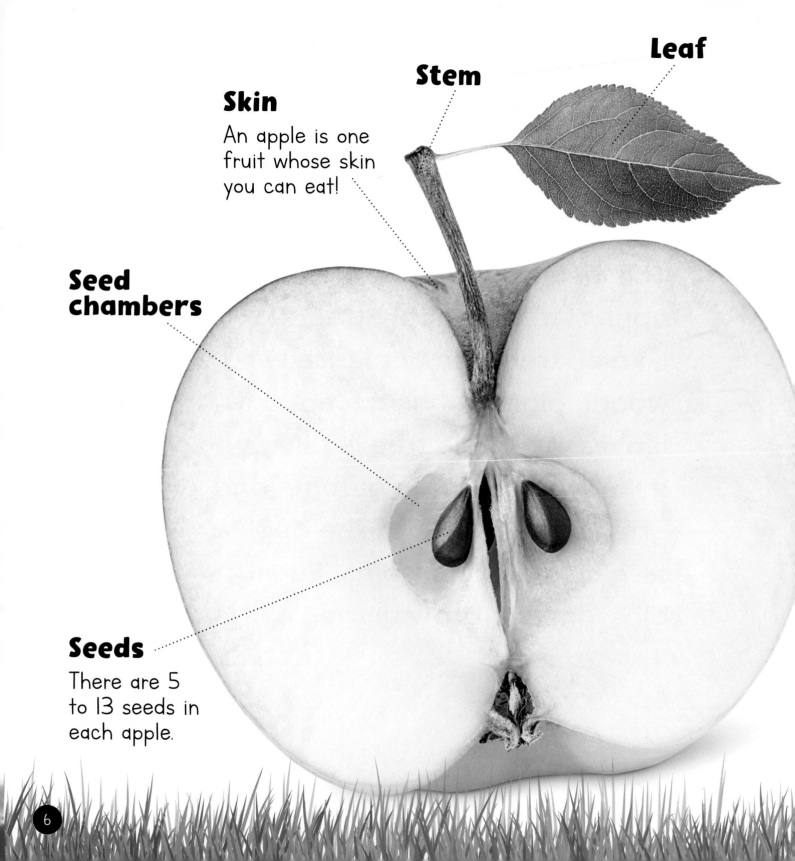

Leaf

Stem

Skin
An apple is one
fruit whose skin
you can eat!

**Seed
chambers**

Seeds
There are 5
to 13 seeds in
each apple.

Apples are grown all over the world.

Yummy Fruit

There are many different types of apples. Some are sweet and crunchy. Others are crisp and tart. Apples may have pink, red, yellow, green, or even dark purple skin. But they all have some things in common. Inside each apple, you will find five seed **chambers** that contain the seeds.

It Starts with a Seed

A seed is buried in the soil. When warm weather comes, the seed splits open. A root begins to grow down into the earth. The root takes in water and **nutrients** from the soil. That feeds the stem and the leaves of the growing plant. As the tree gets larger and stronger, so does its root system.

Leaf

Stem

Seed

Root

A baby tree is called a seedling. ▶

The Seedling

The stem continues to grow taller, and more leaves appear. The seedling, or baby tree, needs plenty of food and energy. The tree uses sunlight, air, and water to make food. That process is called **photosynthesis**.

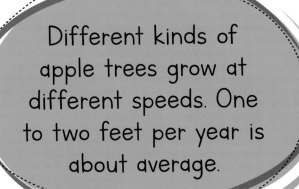

Different kinds of apple trees grow at different speeds. One to two feet per year is about average.

Most apple blossoms start out pale pink. Then they fade to white.

The Blossoms

A few years pass. The tree has grown tall and strong. When spring comes, the tree grows apple blossoms. First, tiny buds cover the branches. Then the buds open into pretty blossoms. Each blossom has five **petals**. A beautiful scent fills the air.

Pistil

The pistil holds the female parts of the flower.

Stamens

These are the male parts of flowers. They make pollen.

Inside the Blossom

Long stamens (STAY-muhnz) are found in the middle of every blossom. They make a yellow powder called pollen. There is also a pistil (PIS-tuhl)

Petals

An apple tree grows blossoms when it reaches five to eight years old. Only then is it able to grow apples.

inside each blossom. Pollen from the blossoms on one apple tree must be carried to pistils on another tree. Only then will the apples start to grow.

Helper Bees

Pollen can't move from blossom to blossom by itself. Sometimes the wind blows it. But most of the time, bees do the job. They collect sweet **nectar** from apple blossoms. When the bees visit the blossoms, pollen sticks to their bodies. The bees fly from tree to tree and from blossom to blossom. Pollen falls off. It tumbles down to the bottom of the pistils. That is called **pollination**.

The sweet smell of the blossom helps attract bees.

▼

The Apple Grows

The apple blossoms have finished their work. The petals fall from the tree. A small fruit begins to grow at the top of the blossom stem. First, the core

forms. Little by little, the rest of the apple takes shape around the core. All summer long, the apples grow larger. In fall, they are finally **ripe**.

Caterpillars leave holes behind when they've been inside an apple.

Aphids are among the most common apple tree pests.

Diseases may also attack the trunk, the leaves, and the fruit.

Birds peck at the apples, leaving holes that can lead to disease.

Apple Tree Enemies

Apples—and apple trees—provide food for many animals. And some of those animals can cause harm. Some insects destroy the tree's leaves. Other pests lay their eggs in the tree. When the eggs **hatch**, caterpillars crawl into the apples. They eat the fruit.

Deer eat apples and may also nibble on the tree's bark.

Crafting the Tastiest Fruit

Most of the apples we eat are not from trees grown from a single seed. Instead, growers join the roots and bottom from one tree to the shoots from another. This process is called grafting. It uses the best parts of each apple plant to make a stronger tree.

Apple trees usually live to be more than 100 years old.

Bottom from one tree

Shoots from another tree

Graft union

Time to Sleep

Winter arrives, and the weather is cold. The branches of the tree are bare. Some apples on the ground begin to rot. That makes the soil rich. Animals may carry away other fallen fruit. New trees can grow from those seeds. The apple trees will sleep all through winter. When spring comes, blossoms and apples will begin to grow all over again.

Apple and Apple Tree Facts

The apple tree is a plant in the rose family. Other plants in that family include roses (pictured), pears, peaches, cherries, and almond trees.

There are more than 7,500 kinds of apples grown in the world. Some popular kinds are Red and Golden Delicious, McIntosh, Honeycrisp, Granny Smith, and Pink Lady.

Most apples are red, green, or golden. But the rare Black Diamond apple (pictured) is a dark purple color. It grows only in the mountains of Tibet, in Asia.

Tiny crab apples, or wild apples, are not so good for eating—they're too tart. But they taste good in jam.

The Hawaii Mountain apple (pictured) is small and has an unusual shape for an apple. It looks more like a pear!

It takes about 36 apples to make one gallon of apple cider.

Apples float in water. That's because they have so much air inside them.

Growing Up from Seed to Apple

Apples are grown on every continent except Antarctica. Each yummy fruit grows on a tree that started from a seed.

Apple
Apples that fall to the ground leave behind seeds that may grow into a new tree.

Seeds
The seeds from inside the apple sink into the ground.

Seedling
The seed grows into a baby tree called a seedling.

Tree
When the tree is five to eight years old, it is ready to grow apples.

Tree with blossoms
In spring, new branches grow and blossoms appear. After the blossoms fall off, apples start to grow.

Tree with apples
In autumn, the apples are ripe. They are ready to eat. Yum!

Glossary

aphids (AY-fidz) tiny insects that feed by sucking the juices from plants

blossoms (BLAH-sumz) flowers on a fruit tree or other plant

chambers (CHAYM-burz) enclosed spaces inside a machine, body, or fruit

deciduous (di-SIJ-oo-uhs) shedding all leaves every year in fall

hatch (HACH) to emerge from an egg, pupa, or chrysalis

nectar (NEK-tur) a sweet liquid from flowers that bees gather and make into honey

nutrients (NOO-tree-uhnts) substances that promote growth and maintain life

petals (PET-uhlz) the colored outer parts of a flower

photosynthesis (foh-toh-SIN-thuh-sis) a chemical process by which plants use energy from the sun to turn water and carbon dioxide into food

pollination (pah-luh-NAY-shuhn) the process by which seeds are created through the transfer of pollen between flowering plants

ripe (RIPE) fully developed or mature; ready to be harvested, picked, or eaten

Index

About the Author

Jodie Shepherd, who also writes under her real name, Leslie Kimmelman, is an award-winning author of dozens of fiction and nonfiction titles for children and was a longtime editor at Sesame Workshop. Apple-picking is one of the things she looks forward to most each year. Last year her family picked more than 80 pounds!